Wego the Wonderful Silkworm

An exciting journey from egg to moth

Jill K. Wilcox

AuthorHouse™
1663 Liberty Drive
Bloomington, IN 47403
www.authorhouse.com
Phone: 833-262-8899

Because of the dynamic nature of the Internet, any web addresses or links contained in this book may have changed
since publication and may no longer be valid. The views expressed in this work are solely those of the author and do
not necessarily reflect the views of the publisher, and the publisher hereby disclaims any responsibility for them.

Any people depicted in stock imagery provided by Getty Images are models,
and such images are being used for illustrative purposes only.
Certain stock imagery © Getty Images.

This book is printed on acid-free paper.

ISBN: 978-1-4259-3510-8 (sc)

Library of Congress Control Number: 2006904483

Print information available on the last page.

Published by AuthorHouse 04/03/2024

authorHOUSE

This journey through life change is dedicated to Mary Wilcox/Kristan who taught me that my life could be whatever I wanted it to be. Thank you Mary for believing in me, encouraging me and supporting me. I love you! Jill

Hi, my name is Wego. My Mom and Dad named me Wego because I was a hairy baby. Were you a hairy baby? Anyway, I was born in a tree with all of my brothers and sisters. I only have 600 brothers and sisters.

We all hatched out of little eggs and that's where my story began. The first thing in my life that I can remember is waking up in a real tight yellow sleeping bag. It was kind of like a cheese puff, so I took a bite out of it and I could see the sky so I climbed out.

Boy was I hungry! I crawled onto a big green blanket and it looked so good that I took a bite out of it too. That blanket was the best thing I had ever tasted so I just kept eating and eating and eating. In fact, I ate the whole blanket all by myself.

I found lots of these green blankets and they were all tasty! I've heard these blankets are called Mulberry leaves but they're just yummy green food to me.

I know this may sound weird, but no matter how much I ate, I was never full. I was so hungry that I didn't even sleep since I couldn't figure out how to eat and sleep at the same time. Sometimes my mouth would get tired but I just couldn't stop eating.

I noticed that I was getting bigger, probably from eating so much. Sometimes my skin would feel so tight that I didn't think I could get any bigger but before I knew it my skin would just peel off and I would have a big baggy one underneath. It didn't even hurt! I was so comfortable in my new roomy skin, but before long that one got tight too. Peeling out of my old skin, and growing into my new one is called molting. So far, I think I've had 4 new baggy skin suits.

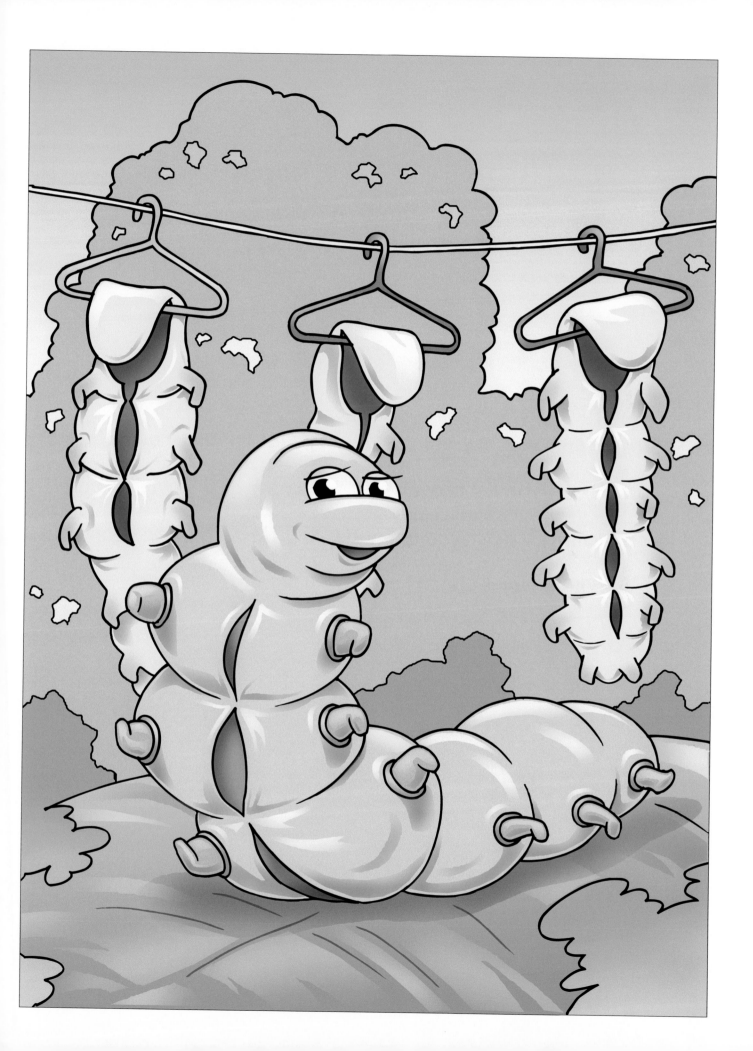

As you can see, my skin is pretty tight right now. I have grown 10,000 times bigger than I was when I was a baby. How big will you be if you grow 10,000 times bigger than you were when you were born?

Lately, I haven't been so hungry. I'm not sure why but I just feel kind of tired. I think I'm going to take a nap but I don't have anywhere safe to sleep. I sure wish I had that snuggly cheese puff that I hatched out of but I don't think I will fit in there anymore. Do you know where I could take a nap?

Hey, I have an idea. I will make myself a new, big, puffy sleeping bag. I have these two little holes under my mouth and this string called silk comes out of them. I bet I could use the silk to build a cozy sleeping place. I'm going to start wrapping the string all around my body. This might take a while but when I'm done I'll be inside a soft, cushy sleeping bag called a cocoon.

Phew, I'm finally done making my cocoon. I'm really tired now. Do you mind if I take a short nap?

Yawn. I feel so much better now. I guess all I needed was a little nap. Hey, why are you looking at me like that?

Let me look in the mirror. WOW! I don't look like Wego anymore do I? I feel the same inside but I sure do look different. I look just like my Mom and Dad! I'm so beautiful. My soft white fur feels so nice. My antennas look like a cool little hairdo! I guess I'm all grown up now. You may not change the way you look as much as I have but you'll grow up like me someday too.

I have to go now. It's time for me to become a Daddy and have little "Wegos" of my own. I'll see you later!

Vocabulary Words included at end of book

Wego- the Japanese word meaning "hairy baby". This is what they call sikworms in Japan, the leading country for silk production.

Mulberry leaves- the primary food for silkworms

Molting- the shedding of the old, tight skin, to allow for growth. A new bigger skin is underneath the old tight one.

Cocoon- the covering that the silkworm builds around itself during the pupa stage. The silkworm (the larva stage) becomes the pupa stage while in the cocoon. The moth (the adult stage) hatches out of the cocoon.

Metamorphosis- describes the change from egg to larva to pupa to adult. Found in moths and butterflies.

About the Author

Jill Wilcox lives in Lakewood, California with her husband and two children. She has been teaching hands-on science classes through her business SCIENCE-2-U, since 1998. "I love that 'Ah-ha" moment when you see a child really understand an idea for the first time. Wego is able to open that door, to one of nature's most important processes."